MASTERING OET SPEAKING : RARE AND SIMPLE OET ROLE PLAYS FOR GUARANTEED SUCCESS

Jobin Thomas

Jobins Training

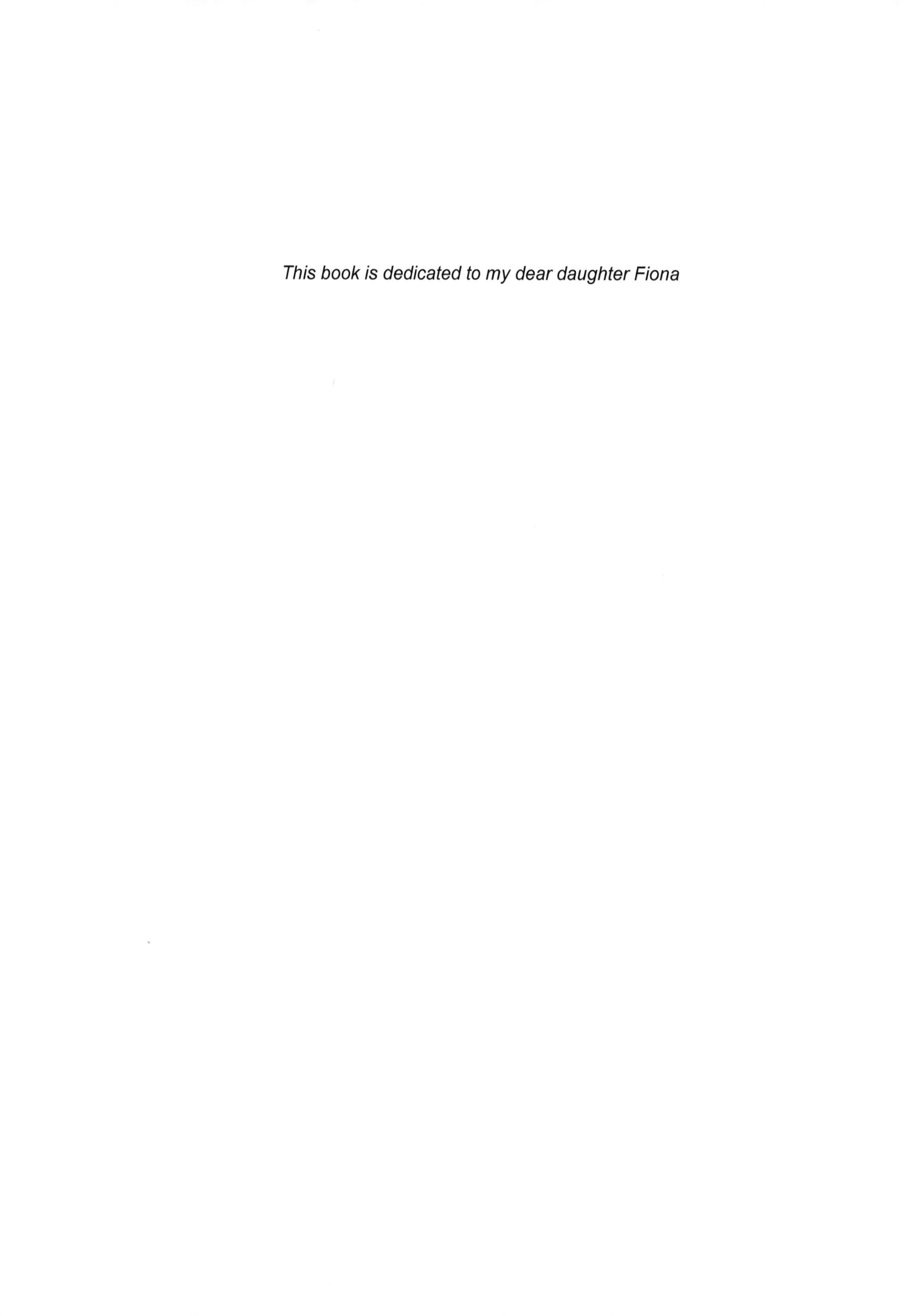

This book is dedicated to my dear daughter Fiona

CONTENTS

TABLE OF CONTENTS

The OET (Occupational English Test) Speaking sub-test is designed to assess the English language proficiency of healthcare professionals in a clinical context. Here's an overview of the format:

OVERVIEW OF OET SPEAKING SUB-TEST

1. Duration: Approximately 20 minutes
2. Structure: Consists of two role plays
3. Participants: One test taker and one interlocutor (a role-player who acts as a patient or a relative)

FORMAT DETAILS

1. Introduction (2-3 minutes)

- Purpose: To make the test taker comfortable and establish a context for the role plays.
- Process: The interlocutor asks general questions about the test taker's professional background.

2. Role Plays (5 minutes each)

- Number of Role Plays: Two
- Preparation Time: 3 minutes for each role play
- Role Play Duration: 5 minutes each

Preparation for Each Role Play

- Receiving the Role Card: The test taker receives a role card that outlines the scenario, their role, and specific tasks they need to perform.
- Reading and Planning: The test taker has 3 minutes to read the role card and prepare. During this time, they can make notes on the role card.

Conducting the Role Play

- Interaction: The test taker interacts with the interlocutor, who plays the role of a patient, a patient's relative, or a caregiver.
- Focus: The test taker must demonstrate their ability to communicate effectively, gather information, provide information, and offer support.

ROLE PLAY CARD CONTENT

Each role play card provides:

- Background Information: The context of the scenario.
- Role and Task: The specific role of the test taker and the tasks they need to complete during the role play.
- Hints and Suggestions: Sometimes, the card includes hints or suggestions to guide the test taker.

KEY SKILLS ASSESSED

1. Clinical Communication Skills:
   - Building rapport with the patient
   - Gathering information through effective questioning
   - Providing clear explanations and information
   - Offering reassurance and demonstrating empathy
2. Language Skills:
   - Using appropriate language for the situation
   - Managing the conversation flow
   - Ensuring clarity and accuracy in communication

SCORING CRITERIA

The speaking sub-test is scored based on:

1. Intelligibility: Pronunciation, intonation, and fluency.
2. Fluency: The flow of speech and the ability to express ideas without undue hesitation.
3. Appropriateness: Use of suitable language and tone for the clinical context.
4. Resources of Grammar and Expression: Range and accuracy of grammatical structures and vocabulary.
5. Relationship Building: Ability to establish a connection and build rapport with the patient.
6. Understanding and Incorporating Patient's Perspective: Showing empathy and understanding of the patient's feelings and concerns.
7. Providing Structure: Organizing information logically and clearly.
8. Information Gathering and Giving: Effectiveness in eliciting and providing information.

EXAMPLE OF A ROLE PLAY SCENARIO

Role Play Card Example:

Background: You are a nurse in a community health clinic. A 45-year-old patient has come to the clinic feeling very anxious about their upcoming surgery.

Tasks:

1. Greet the patient and introduce yourself.
2. Acknowledge the patient's feelings and show empathy.
3. Explain the surgery process in simple terms.
4. Reassure the patient by discussing the safety measures and success rates.
5. Offer strategies to manage anxiety, such as breathing exercises or speaking with a counselor.

DURING THE ROLE PLAY

Nurse (You): "Hello, my name is [Your Name], and I'll be your nurse today. I understand you're feeling anxious about your upcoming surgery. That's completely understandable. Many patients feel this way before a procedure. Let's talk about what's worrying you, and I'll do my best to help you feel more comfortable."

Patient (Interlocutor): "I'm just really scared about the surgery. I don't know what to expect."

Nurse (You): "It's normal to feel scared about something new. Let me explain what will happen during the surgery. First, you will... [briefly describe the steps]. We have a very experienced team, and we'll take excellent care of you. Your safety is our top priority. Do you have any questions about the procedure?"

ROLE PLAY CARD 1: HUNTINGTON'S DISEASE

Setting: Neurology Clinic

Patient: You are a 45-year-old diagnosed with Huntington's disease. You are concerned about the progressive nature of the disease and its impact on your family.

Task:

- Express concerns about the progression and symptoms of Huntington's disease.
- Ask about available treatments and their effectiveness.
- Enquire about the genetic implications for your children.
- Ask about support resources for families affected by Huntington's disease.

Setting: Neurology Clinic

Nurse: A 45-year-old patient has been diagnosed with Huntington's disease and is worried about the progression and impact on their family.

Task:

- Reassure the patient and explain the progression of the disease.
- Discuss available treatments and their effectiveness.
- Explain the genetic implications for the patient's children.
- Provide information on support resources for families.

ROLE PLAY CARD 2: CYSTIC FIBROSIS

Setting: Pulmonology Clinic

Patient: You are a 30-year-old living with cystic fibrosis. You are experiencing increasing respiratory issues and are worried about managing your condition.

Task:

- Express concerns about worsening respiratory symptoms.
- Ask about advanced treatment options.
- Enquire about daily management strategies to improve quality of life.
- Ask about life expectancy and future planning.

Setting: Pulmonology Clinic

Nurse: A 30-year-old patient with cystic fibrosis is experiencing worsening respiratory issues and is concerned about managing their condition.

Task:

- Reassure the patient and validate their concerns.
- Discuss advanced treatment options for cystic fibrosis.
- Suggest daily management strategies to improve quality of life.
- Provide information on life expectancy and future planning.

ROLE PLAY CARD 3: MARFAN SYNDROME

Setting: Cardiology Clinic

Patient: You are a 25-year-old diagnosed with Marfan syndrome. You are worried about the cardiovascular complications associated with the condition.

Task:

- Express concerns about cardiovascular complications.
- Ask about monitoring and managing the condition.
- Enquire about lifestyle modifications to reduce risks.
- Ask about genetic counseling for family planning.

Setting: Cardiology Clinic

Nurse: A 25-year-old patient with Marfan syndrome is worried about cardiovascular complications and managing the condition.

Task:

- Reassure the patient and explain cardiovascular risks.
- Discuss monitoring and management strategies.
- Suggest lifestyle modifications to reduce risks.
- Provide information on genetic counseling for family planning.

ROLE PLAY CARD 4: WILSON'S DISEASE

Setting: Hepatology Clinic

Patient: You are a 35-year-old diagnosed with Wilson's disease, a rare genetic disorder that causes copper accumulation in your body. You are concerned about liver damage and neurological symptoms.

Task:

- Express concerns about liver damage and neurological symptoms.
- Ask about treatment options and their effectiveness.
- Enquire about dietary restrictions and lifestyle changes.
- Ask about long-term management and prognosis.

Setting: Hepatology Clinic

Nurse: A 35-year-old patient has been diagnosed with Wilson's disease and is concerned about liver damage and neurological symptoms.

Task:

- Reassure the patient and explain the nature of Wilson's disease.
- Discuss treatment options and their effectiveness.
- Provide information on dietary restrictions and lifestyle changes.
- Explain long-term management and prognosis.

ROLE PLAY CARD 5: GAUCHER DISEASE

Setting: Hematology Clinic

Patient: You are a 40-year-old with Gaucher disease, a rare genetic disorder affecting your spleen and bones. You are worried about managing symptoms and long-term effects.

Task:

- Express concerns about spleen and bone complications.
- Ask about available treatments and their side effects.
- Enquire about managing pain and other symptoms.
- Ask about support resources and long-term prognosis.

Setting: Hematology Clinic

Nurse: A 40-year-old patient with Gaucher disease is worried about managing spleen and bone complications and the long-term effects of the condition.

Task:

- Reassure the patient and explain Gaucher disease.
- Discuss available treatments and their side effects.
- Suggest strategies to manage pain and other symptoms.
- Provide information on support resources and prognosis.

ROLE PLAY CARD 6: AMYLOIDOSIS

Setting: Internal Medicine Clinic

Patient: You are a 55-year-old diagnosed with amyloidosis, a rare condition where abnormal protein deposits build up in your organs. You are concerned about the impact on your heart and kidneys.

Task:

- Express concerns about organ damage due to amyloidosis.
- Ask about treatment options and their effectiveness.
- Enquire about managing symptoms and improving quality of life.
- Ask about support resources for patients with amyloidosis.

Setting: Internal Medicine Clinic

Nurse: A 55-year-old patient has been diagnosed with amyloidosis and is concerned about the impact on their heart and kidneys.

Task:

- Reassure the patient and explain amyloidosis.
- Discuss treatment options and their effectiveness.
- Suggest strategies to manage symptoms and improve quality of life.
- Provide information on support resources.

ROLE PLAY CARD 7: ADDISON'S DISEASE

Setting: Endocrinology Clinic

Patient: You are a 45-year-old diagnosed with Addison's disease, a rare disorder affecting your adrenal glands. You are worried about managing the condition and potential crises.

Task:

- Express concerns about managing Addison's disease and adrenal crises.
- Ask about medication and treatment plans.
- Enquire about recognizing and handling adrenal crises.
- Ask about lifestyle modifications and support resources.

Setting: Endocrinology Clinic

Nurse: A 45-year-old patient with Addison's disease is worried about managing the condition and potential adrenal crises.

Task:

- Reassure the patient and explain Addison's disease.
- Discuss medication and treatment plans.
- Provide information on recognizing and handling adrenal crises.
- Suggest lifestyle modifications and support resources.

ROLE PLAY CARD 8: SCLERODERMA

Setting: Rheumatology Clinic

Patient: You are a 50-year-old diagnosed with scleroderma, a rare autoimmune disease that causes hardening of the skin and connective tissues. You are concerned about managing symptoms and preventing complications.

Task:

- Express concerns about the progression and symptoms of scleroderma.
- Ask about treatment options and their effectiveness.
- Enquire about managing daily activities and preventing complications.
- Ask about support groups for scleroderma patients.

Setting: Rheumatology Clinic

Nurse: A 50-year-old patient with scleroderma is concerned about managing symptoms and preventing complications.

Task:

- Reassure the patient and explain scleroderma.
- Discuss treatment options and their effectiveness.
- Suggest strategies for managing daily activities and preventing complications.
- Provide information on support groups for scleroderma patients.

ROLE PLAY CARD 9: FABRY DISEASE

Setting: Nephrology Clinic

Patient: You are a 35-year-old diagnosed with Fabry disease, a rare genetic disorder affecting your kidneys and cardiovascular system. You are worried about the impact on your health and family.

Task:

- Express concerns about kidney and cardiovascular complications.
- Ask about treatment options and their effectiveness.
- Enquire about genetic counseling for family planning.
- Ask about support resources for managing Fabry disease.

Setting: Nephrology Clinic

Nurse: A 35-year-old patient with Fabry disease is worried about kidney and cardiovascular complications and the impact on their family.

Task:

- Reassure the patient and explain Fabry disease.
- Discuss treatment options and their effectiveness.
- Provide information on genetic counseling for family planning.
- Suggest support resources for managing Fabry disease.

ROLE PLAY CARD 10: EHLERS-DANLOS SYNDROME

Setting: Orthopedic Clinic

Patient: You are a 30-year-old diagnosed with Ehlers-Danlos syndrome, a rare connective tissue disorder. You are worried about joint pain, dislocations, and managing daily life.

Task:

- Express concerns about joint pain and frequent dislocations.
- Ask about treatment options and pain management.
- Enquire about exercises and activities to strengthen joints.
- Ask about support resources for living with Ehlers-Danlos syndrome.

Setting: Orthopedic Clinic

Nurse: A 30-year-old patient with Ehlers-Danlos syndrome is concerned about joint pain, frequent dislocations, and managing daily life.

Task:

- Reassure the patient and explain Ehlers-Danlos syndrome.
- Discuss treatment options and pain management.
- Suggest exercises and activities to strengthen joints.
- Provide information on support resources.

These role play cards cover a range of rare conditions and address complex concerns, providing a high level of difficulty for OET exam preparation.

Approaching these high-difficulty role plays as a nurse requires a combination of strong communication skills, empathy, and clinical knowledge. Here's a guide on how to handle each role play scenario:

NOW EXPLAIN HOW TO
APPROACH THESE ROLE
PLAY AS NURSE

ROLE PLAY CARD 1: HUNTINGTON'S DISEASE

Approach:

1. Empathy and Reassurance: Start by expressing empathy for the patient's situation. Reassure them that their concerns are valid and that you are there to help.
2. Provide Information: Explain the nature of Huntington's disease, including its genetic basis and progressive nature.
3. Discuss Treatment: Outline available treatment options, focusing on symptom management and support services.
4. Genetic Counseling: Discuss the implications for family members and the importance of genetic counseling.
5. Support Resources: Offer information about support groups and resources for patients and families.

ROLE PLAY CARD 2: CYSTIC FIBROSIS

Approach:

1. Empathy and Validation: Acknowledge the patient's struggles with respiratory symptoms and their impact on quality of life.
2. Detailed Explanation: Provide detailed information about cystic fibrosis and its effects on the body.
3. Advanced Treatments: Discuss advanced treatment options, including medications, physiotherapy, and possible surgical interventions.
4. Daily Management: Suggest daily management strategies, such as chest physiotherapy and nutritional support.
5. Future Planning: Address concerns about life expectancy and the importance of regular follow-ups.

ROLE PLAY CARD 3: MARFAN SYNDROME

Approach:

1. Empathy and Understanding: Show empathy for the patient's concerns about cardiovascular complications.
2. Clear Information: Explain Marfan syndrome, its symptoms, and potential risks, particularly regarding cardiovascular health.
3. Monitoring and Management: Discuss the importance of regular monitoring, including echocardiograms and other assessments.
4. Lifestyle Modifications: Suggest lifestyle changes, such as avoiding strenuous activities, to reduce risks.
5. Genetic Counseling: Provide information on genetic counseling for family planning.

ROLE PLAY CARD 4: WILSON'S DISEASE

Approach:

1. Empathy and Support: Express empathy for the patient's worries about liver and neurological complications.
2. Educational Explanation: Explain Wilson's disease, including how copper accumulates in the body and affects organs.
3. Treatment Options: Discuss treatment options, such as chelation therapy and dietary changes to limit copper intake.
4. Dietary and Lifestyle Advice: Provide detailed dietary advice and lifestyle modifications.
5. Long-term Management: Explain the importance of ongoing management and regular medical check-ups.

ROLE PLAY CARD 5: GAUCHER DISEASE

Approach:

1. Empathy and Validation: Acknowledge the patient's concerns about spleen and bone complications.
2. Disease Education: Explain Gaucher disease, its symptoms, and how it affects the body.
3. Treatment Discussion: Discuss treatment options, including enzyme replacement therapy and their side effects.
4. Symptom Management: Suggest strategies for managing pain and other symptoms.
5. Support and Prognosis: Provide information on support resources and discuss the prognosis.

ROLE PLAY CARD 6: AMYLOIDOSIS

Approach:

1. Empathy and Reassurance: Show empathy for the patient's concerns about organ damage.
2. Detailed Explanation: Explain amyloidosis, how protein deposits affect organs, and the potential impact.
3. Treatment Options: Discuss treatment options, including medications and possible interventions to manage organ damage.
4. Symptom Management: Provide strategies to manage symptoms and improve quality of life.
5. Support Resources: Offer information on support resources and patient groups.

ROLE PLAY CARD 7: ADDISON'S DISEASE

Approach:

1. Empathy and Understanding: Acknowledge the patient's concerns about managing Addison's disease and potential crises.
2. Disease Education: Explain Addison's disease, its symptoms, and how it affects the adrenal glands.
3. Treatment Plan: Discuss medication options and the importance of adhering to treatment plans.
4. Crisis Management: Educate the patient on recognizing and handling adrenal crises, including emergency measures.
5. Lifestyle and Support: Suggest lifestyle modifications and provide information on support resources.

ROLE PLAY CARD 8: SCLERODERMA

Approach:

1. Empathy and Support: Show empathy for the patient's concerns about the progression of scleroderma.
2. Disease Explanation: Explain scleroderma, its symptoms, and potential complications.
3. Treatment Options: Discuss available treatments and their effectiveness in managing symptoms.
4. Daily Management: Suggest strategies for managing daily activities and preventing complications.
5. Support Groups: Provide information on support groups and resources for patients with scleroderma.

ROLE PLAY CARD 9: FABRY DISEASE

Approach:

1. Empathy and Validation: Acknowledge the patient's concerns about kidney and cardiovascular complications.
2. Disease Information: Explain Fabry disease, its symptoms, and how it affects the body.
3. Treatment Discussion: Discuss treatment options, including enzyme replacement therapy and their effectiveness.
4. Genetic Counseling: Provide information on genetic counseling for family planning.
5. Support Resources: Offer information on support resources and patient groups.

ROLE PLAY CARD 10: EHLERS-DANLOS SYNDROME

Approach:

1. Empathy and Understanding: Show empathy for the patient's concerns about joint pain and dislocations.
2. Detailed Explanation: Explain Ehlers-Danlos syndrome, its symptoms, and how it affects connective tissues.
3. Treatment and Pain Management: Discuss treatment options and strategies for managing pain.
4. Exercise and Activities: Suggest exercises and activities to strengthen joints and improve stability.
5. Support Resources: Provide information on support resources and patient groups.

GENERAL TIPS FOR ALL ROLE PLAYS:

- Active Listening: Show that you are listening by nodding, maintaining eye contact, and paraphrasing the patient's concerns.
- Empathy: Always start by acknowledging the patient's feelings and concerns. Empathy helps build trust and rapport.
- Clarity: Use clear, non-technical language to explain medical conditions and treatments. Ensure the patient understands the information.
- Reassurance: Reassure the patient that they are not alone and that help is available. This can alleviate anxiety and build confidence.
- Information: Provide comprehensive information about the condition, treatment options, and support resources.
- Encouragement: Encourage the patient to ask questions and express their concerns. Provide them with the opportunity to discuss their worries.
- Follow-up: Mention the importance of follow-up appointments and continuous monitoring to manage their condition effectively.

ROLE PLAY CARD 1: ASTHMA MANAGEMENT

Setting: General Practice Clinic

Patient: You are a 35-year-old office worker experiencing frequent asthma attacks. You are worried because your current medication doesn't seem to be effective. You are anxious about how this might affect your work and daily life.

Task:

- Express concerns about the frequency of asthma attacks.
- Ask if the current medication needs to be changed.
- Enquire about lifestyle changes that could help manage asthma.
- Ask about the possibility of seeing a specialist.

Setting: General Practice Clinic

Nurse: A 35-year-old office worker is under your care, complaining about frequent asthma attacks. The patient is anxious about their condition affecting their work and daily life.

Task:

- Reassure the patient about the manageability of asthma.
- Discuss the importance of adhering to the prescribed medication regimen.
- Suggest lifestyle changes to reduce asthma triggers.
- Discuss the referral process to a specialist.

ROLE PLAY CARD 2: DIABETES MANAGEMENT

Setting: Diabetes Clinic

Patient: You are a 50-year-old recently diagnosed with Type 2 diabetes. You are unsure about how to manage your condition and are worried about the long-term implications.

Task:

- Express confusion about dietary restrictions.
- Ask about the importance of exercise in managing diabetes.
- Enquire about the potential complications if diabetes is not managed properly.
- Ask about support groups or resources available for diabetic patients.

Setting: Diabetes Clinic

Nurse: A 50-year-old patient has been recently diagnosed with Type 2 diabetes. The patient is unsure about managing the condition and worried about long-term implications.

Task:

- Explain the dietary restrictions and their importance.
- Emphasize the role of exercise in managing diabetes.
- Educate the patient about potential complications if diabetes is not managed.

- Provide information on support groups and resources.

ROLE PLAY CARD 3: POST-SURGICAL CARE

Setting: Surgical Ward

Patient: You are a 40-year-old recovering from knee surgery. You are experiencing pain and are concerned about your mobility and recovery timeline.

Task:

- Express concerns about post-surgical pain and mobility.
- Ask about the expected recovery timeline.
- Enquire about exercises or activities to aid recovery.
- Ask about pain management options.

Setting: Surgical Ward

Nurse: A 40-year-old patient is recovering from knee surgery and is concerned about pain, mobility, and the recovery timeline.

Task:

- Reassure the patient about the normalcy of post-surgical pain.
- Discuss the expected recovery timeline.
- Suggest exercises or activities to aid recovery.
- Explain pain management options.

ROLE PLAY CARD 4: MENTAL HEALTH

Setting: Mental Health Clinic

Patient: You are a 28-year-old experiencing symptoms of depression. You feel overwhelmed and are struggling to cope with daily tasks.

Task:

- Express feelings of overwhelm and inability to cope.
- Ask about treatment options for depression.
- Enquire about counseling or therapy sessions.
- Ask about lifestyle changes that could help improve mental health.

Setting: Mental Health Clinic

Nurse: A 28-year-old patient is experiencing symptoms of depression and is struggling to cope with daily tasks.

Task:

- Reassure the patient and validate their feelings.
- Discuss treatment options for depression.
- Provide information about counseling or therapy sessions.
- Suggest lifestyle changes to improve mental health.

ROLE PLAY CARD 5: HYPERTENSION MANAGEMENT

Setting: Cardiology Clinic

Patient: You are a 60-year-old with newly diagnosed hypertension. You are concerned about the impact of hypertension on your overall health and lifestyle.

Task:

- Express concerns about the health implications of hypertension.
- Ask about dietary changes to manage hypertension.
- Enquire about the necessity of medication.
- Ask about the importance of regular exercise.

Setting: Cardiology Clinic

Nurse: A 60-year-old patient has been newly diagnosed with hypertension and is concerned about the impact on overall health and lifestyle.

Task:

- Reassure the patient about managing hypertension effectively.
- Discuss dietary changes to help manage hypertension.
- Explain the necessity and benefits of medication.
- Emphasize the importance of regular exercise.

ROLE PLAY CARD 6: ALLERGY MANAGEMENT

Setting: Allergy Clinic

Patient: You are a 25-year-old experiencing severe allergic reactions to pollen. You are frustrated because it affects your daily activities and social life.

Task:

- Express frustration about the impact of allergies on daily life.
- Ask about long-term management options.
- Enquire about medication to control symptoms.
- Ask about lifestyle modifications to reduce exposure to allergens.

Setting: Allergy Clinic

Nurse: A 25-year-old patient is experiencing severe allergic reactions to pollen, affecting daily activities and social life.

Task:

- Reassure the patient and acknowledge their frustration.
- Discuss long-term management options for allergies.
- Explain medication options to control symptoms.
- Suggest lifestyle modifications to reduce exposure to allergens.

ROLE PLAY CARD 7: POSTPARTUM CARE

Setting: Postnatal Ward

Patient: You are a 32-year-old who has recently given birth. You are experiencing postpartum depression and struggling to adjust to motherhood.

Task:

- Express feelings of sadness and difficulty adjusting.
- Ask about support available for postpartum depression.
- Enquire about strategies to cope with the new responsibilities.
- Ask about the possibility of joining a new mothers' support group.

Setting: Postnatal Ward

Nurse: A 32-year-old patient has recently given birth and is experiencing postpartum depression, struggling to adjust to motherhood.

Task:

- Reassure the patient and validate their feelings.
- Provide information about support available for postpartum depression.
- Discuss strategies to cope with new responsibilities.
- Suggest joining a new mothers' support group.

ROLE PLAY CARD 8: CHRONIC PAIN MANAGEMENT

Setting: Pain Management Clinic

Patient: You are a 45-year-old with chronic back pain. You are frustrated because it affects your ability to work and enjoy life.

Task:

- Express frustration about the impact of chronic pain.
- Ask about treatment options to manage pain.
- Enquire about alternative therapies.
- Ask about lifestyle changes to reduce pain.

Setting: Pain Management Clinic

Nurse: A 45-year-old patient is experiencing chronic back pain, affecting their ability to work and enjoy life.

Task:

- Reassure the patient and acknowledge their frustration.
- Discuss treatment options to manage chronic pain.
- Provide information about alternative therapies.
- Suggest lifestyle changes to help reduce pain.

ROLE PLAY CARD 9: PEDIATRIC CARE

Setting: Pediatric Clinic

Patient: You are a parent of a 3-year-old with recurring ear infections. You are worried about the impact on your child's hearing and overall health.

Task:

- Express concerns about the frequency of ear infections.
- Ask about the potential impact on your child's hearing.
- Enquire about preventive measures.
- Ask about the necessity of antibiotics and their side effects.

Setting: Pediatric Clinic

Nurse: A parent of a 3-year-old with recurring ear infections is worried about the impact on the child's hearing and overall health.

Task:

- Reassure the parent about the manageability of ear infections.
- Discuss the potential impact on hearing and health.
- Provide preventive measures to reduce infections.
- Explain the necessity and side effects of antibiotics.

ROLE PLAY CARD 10: GERIATRIC CARE

Setting: Geriatric Ward

Patient: You are an 80-year-old with mobility issues and arthritis. You are worried about losing independence and managing daily activities.

Task:

- Express concerns about losing independence.
- Ask about ways to manage arthritis pain.
- Enquire about mobility aids.
- Ask about support services available for the elderly.

Setting: Geriatric Ward

Nurse: An 80-year-old patient with mobility issues and arthritis is worried about losing independence and managing daily activities.

Task:

- Reassure the patient and acknowledge their concerns.
- Discuss ways to manage arthritis pain.
- Suggest appropriate mobility aids.
- Provide information about support services available for the elderly.

UNDERSTANDING THE ROLE PLAY STRUCTURE

1. Introduction:
   - Read the Role Card Carefully: Understand the scenario, your role, and the patient's situation.
   - Identify Key Points: Note the main tasks you need to accomplish during the role play.
2. Warm-Up:
   - Greet the Patient: Use a warm and professional greeting.
   - Introduce Yourself: Clearly state your name and role.
   - Confirm Patient Details: Verify the patient's identity and reason for the visit.

EFFECTIVE COMMUNICATION STRATEGIES

1. Empathy and Rapport:
   - Show Empathy: Acknowledge the patient's feelings and concerns.
   - Build Rapport: Use active listening, maintain eye contact, and use the patient's name.
2. Clear and Structured Communication:
   - Explain Clearly: Use simple language to explain medical terms and procedures.
   - Check Understanding: Ask the patient to repeat the information to ensure they understand.
3. Gathering Information:
   - Open-Ended Questions: Start with questions that allow the patient to provide more detailed responses.
   - Closed-Ended Questions: Use these for specific information.
4. Providing Information and Advice:
   - Be Specific: Give clear instructions and information tailored to the patient's situation.
   - Use Examples: Provide examples or analogies to make information more relatable.

HANDLING COMMON SCENARIOS

1. Breaking Bad News:
   - Be Sensitive: Approach the topic gently and provide support.
   - Offer Support: Discuss next steps and offer emotional support.
2. Dealing with Anxious or Angry Patients:
   - Stay Calm: Maintain a calm and professional demeanor.
   - Listen Actively: Allow the patient to express their feelings and acknowledge their emotions.
3. Patient Education:
   - Simplify Information: Break down complex information into manageable parts.
   - Use Visual Aids: Where possible, use diagrams or written materials to help explain.

PRACTICE AND PREPARATION

1. Role-Play Practice:
   - Practice with Peers: Regularly practice role plays with classmates or colleagues.
   - Record Yourself: Record your role plays and review them to identify areas for improvement.
2. Seek Feedback:
   - Get Constructive Criticism: Ask for feedback from peers, mentors, or language instructors.
   - Implement Feedback: Work on the areas of improvement suggested by others.
3. Familiarize Yourself with Common Scenarios:
   - Study Common Cases: Learn about typical scenarios that are relevant to your healthcare profession.
   - Prepare for Unexpected Situations: Think about how you would handle less common situations as well.

DURING THE ROLE PLAY

1. Time Management:
   - Keep Track of Time: Be aware of the time limit and manage your role play accordingly.
   - Prioritize Tasks: Focus on completing the essential tasks outlined in the role card.
2. Stay Focused:
   - Stick to the Scenario: Don't deviate from the role play scenario.
   - Stay in Character: Maintain your professional role throughout the interaction.

AFTER THE ROLE PLAY

1. Self-Reflection:
   - Review Your Performance: Reflect on what went well and what could be improved.
   - Plan for Improvement: Develop a plan to address any weaknesses.

By following these tips and strategies, you can approach the OET Role Play with confidence and demonstrate your ability to communicate effectively in a healthcare setting.

STEPS TO HANDLE A SAD PATIENT

1. Greet and Introduce Yourself
2. Acknowledge Their Feelings
3. Show Empathy and Support
4. Encourage Expression
5. Provide Reassurance
6. Offer Practical Help
7. Plan Follow-Up and Continued Support
8. Close the Conversation

EXAMPLE ROLE PLAY SCRIPT

Scenario:
A patient has received upsetting news about their health and is feeling very sad.

Role Play Card Example:
Background: You are a nurse in a community clinic. A 50-year-old patient has just received news of a chronic illness diagnosis and is feeling very sad.

Tasks:

1. Greet the patient and introduce yourself.
2. Acknowledge the patient's feelings and show empathy.
3. Encourage the patient to express their feelings.
4. Reassure the patient about the support available.
5. Offer practical advice and information about managing the illness.
6. Plan follow-up appointments or support sessions.

DETAILED SCRIPT

Greeting and Introduction
Nurse (You): "Hello [Patient's Name], my name is [Your Name], and I'm your nurse today. I understand that you've received some upsetting news about your health. How are you feeling right now?"

Acknowledging Their Feelings
Patient: "I'm feeling really sad and overwhelmed. I don't know how to handle this."

Nurse (You): "I'm really sorry to hear that you're feeling this way. It's completely understandable to feel sad and overwhelmed after receiving such news."

Showing Empathy and Support
Nurse (You): "It's important to acknowledge your feelings. Many people feel the same way when they get news like this. You're not alone in this."

Encouraging Expression
Nurse (You): "Would you like to talk more about what's making you feel this way? Sometimes it helps to share your thoughts and feelings."

Patient: "I'm just worried about how this will affect my life and my family."

Providing Reassurance
Nurse (You): "I can understand why you would be worried. It's a big change, but we're here to support you. There are many resources and treatments available that can help manage your condition and improve your quality of life."

Offering Practical Help

Nurse (You): "Let's talk about some practical steps we can take. For example, we can schedule regular check-ups to monitor your condition, and I can provide you with information about support groups and counseling services. These can be very helpful."

Planning Follow-Up and Continued Support
Nurse (You): "We'll also make sure to follow up with you regularly. How about we set up a follow-up appointment for next week? This way, we can check in on how you're feeling and adjust your care plan as needed."

Closing the Conversation
Nurse (You): "Remember, you don't have to go through this alone. We're here to support you every step of the way. If you have any questions or just need someone to talk to, please don't hesitate to reach out."

KEY PHRASES TO USE

- "I'm really sorry to hear that you're feeling this way."
- "It's completely understandable to feel sad and overwhelmed."
- "You're not alone in this."
- "Would you like to talk more about what's making you feel this way?"
- "We're here to support you."
- "There are many resources and treatments available."
- "Let's talk about some practical steps we can take."
- "How about we set up a follow-up appointment for next week?"
- "Remember, you don't have to go through this alone."

By using these strategies and phrases, you can effectively handle a sad patient during an OET role play, demonstrating empathy, providing reassurance, and offering practical support.

Handling a depressed patient during an OET role play requires sensitivity, empathy, and effective communication. Here's how to approach this scenario with appropriate language and actions:

STEPS TO HANDLE A DEPRESSED PATIENT

1. Greet and Introduce Yourself
2. Acknowledge Their Feelings
3. Show Empathy and Support
4. Encourage Expression
5. Provide Reassurance and Information
6. Offer Practical Help and Resources
7. Plan Follow-Up and Continued Support
8. Close the Conversation

EXAMPLE ROLE PLAY SCRIPT

Scenario:
A patient has been feeling very depressed due to chronic pain and is struggling to cope.

Role Play Card Example:
Background: You are a nurse in a primary care clinic. A 45-year-old patient has been experiencing chronic pain and is feeling very depressed. They have come to see you for help.

Tasks:

1. Greet the patient and introduce yourself.
2. Acknowledge the patient's feelings and show empathy.
3. Encourage the patient to express their feelings.
4. Reassure the patient about the support available.
5. Offer practical advice and information about managing depression.
6. Plan follow-up appointments or support sessions.

DETAILED SCRIPT

Greeting and Introduction

Nurse (You): "Hello [Patient's Name], my name is [Your Name], and I'm your nurse today. I understand you've been going through a difficult time with your chronic pain. How are you feeling today?"

Acknowledging Their Feelings

Patient: "I'm feeling really down and depressed. I don't know how to deal with this anymore."

Nurse (You): "I'm really sorry to hear that you're feeling this way. It's completely understandable to feel depressed when dealing with chronic pain."

Showing Empathy and Support

Nurse (You): "It's important to acknowledge your feelings. You're going through a lot, and it's okay to feel this way. You're not alone in this."

Encouraging Expression

Nurse (You): "Would you like to talk more about what's been going on and how you're feeling? Sometimes sharing your thoughts can help."

Patient: "I just feel so hopeless. The pain never seems to go away."

Providing Reassurance and Information

Nurse (You): "I can understand why you're feeling hopeless. Chronic pain can be very challenging to deal with. However, there are ways we can help manage both the pain and the depression. We have a range of treatments and support options available."

Offering Practical Help and Resources

Nurse (You): "Let's discuss some steps we can take to help you feel better. We can explore pain management options, such as physical therapy, medications, or alternative treatments. Additionally, we can refer you to a mental health professional who specializes in helping people with chronic pain. Support groups can also be very helpful, as they allow you to connect with others who are going through similar experiences."

Planning Follow-Up and Continued Support
Nurse (You): "We'll also schedule regular follow-up appointments to monitor your progress and adjust your treatment plan as needed. How about we set up a follow-up appointment for next week? This way, we can check in on how you're feeling and make sure you're getting the support you need."

Closing the Conversation
Nurse (You): "Remember, you don't have to go through this alone. We're here to support you every step of the way. If you have any questions or just need to talk, please don't hesitate to reach out. We're here to help you."

KEY PHRASES TO USE

- "I'm really sorry to hear that you're feeling this way."
- "It's completely understandable to feel depressed when dealing with chronic pain."
- "You're not alone in this."
- "Would you like to talk more about what's been going on and how you're feeling?"
- "We have a range of treatments and support options available."
- "Let's discuss some steps we can take to help you feel better."
- "Support groups can also be very helpful."
- "How about we set up a follow-up appointment for next week?"
- "Remember, you don't have to go through this alone."

By using these strategies and phrases, you can effectively handle a depressed patient during an OET role play, demonstrating empathy, providing reassurance, and offering practical support.

Handling an anxious patient during an OET role play requires demonstrating empathy, effective communication, and providing reassurance. Here's how to approach this scenario with appropriate language and actions:

STEPS TO HANDLE AN ANXIOUS PATIENT

1. Greet and Introduce Yourself
2. Acknowledge Their Feelings
3. Show Empathy and Support
4. Encourage Expression
5. Provide Clear and Simple Information
6. Offer Reassurance
7. Suggest Coping Strategies
8. Plan Follow-Up and Continued Support
9. Close the Conversation

EXAMPLE ROLE PLAY SCRIPT

Scenario:
A patient is feeling very anxious about an upcoming medical procedure.

Role Play Card Example:
Background: You are a nurse in a community health clinic. A 45-year-old patient has come to the clinic feeling very anxious about their upcoming surgery.

Tasks:

1. Greet the patient and introduce yourself.
2. Acknowledge the patient's feelings and show empathy.
3. Encourage the patient to express their feelings.
4. Provide clear information about the procedure.
5. Reassure the patient about the safety and success of the procedure.
6. Suggest coping strategies to manage anxiety.
7. Plan follow-up appointments or support sessions.

DETAILED SCRIPT

Greeting and Introduction

Nurse (You): "Hello [Patient's Name], my name is [Your Name], and I'll be your nurse today. I understand you're feeling quite anxious about your upcoming surgery. How are you feeling right now?"

Acknowledging Their Feelings

Patient: "I'm really scared about the surgery. I've never had surgery before, and I don't know what to expect."

Nurse (You): "It's completely normal to feel scared before a surgery, especially if it's your first time. Many people feel the same way."

Showing Empathy and Support

Nurse (You): "I understand that this is a lot to take in, and it's okay to feel anxious. You're not alone, and we're here to support you."

Encouraging Expression

Nurse (You): "Can you tell me more about what's making you feel anxious? Sometimes talking about it can help."

Patient: "I'm worried about the procedure itself and what might go wrong."

Providing Clear and Simple Information

Nurse (You): "Let me explain what will happen during the surgery. First, you will be given anesthesia so you won't feel any pain. The surgical team is very experienced and will take great care of you throughout the procedure. The surgery itself is quite routine and usually takes about an hour."

Offering Reassurance

Nurse (You): "Most patients recover very well after this surgery, and the success rate is very high. Our team is highly skilled, and we'll do everything we can to ensure your safety and comfort."

Suggesting Coping Strategies
Nurse (You): "Many patients find it helpful to practice some relaxation techniques to manage their anxiety. Would you like to try a simple breathing exercise with me now?"

Patient: "Okay, I'll try."

Nurse (You): "Great. Let's take a deep breath in together… and slowly breathe out. Let's do this a few more times. [Guide the patient through a few breaths.] How do you feel now?"

Patient: "A little better, thank you."

Planning Follow-Up and Continued Support
Nurse (You): "I'm glad to hear that. We'll also arrange for a follow-up appointment after your surgery to check on your recovery and address any concerns you might have. If you have any questions or need to talk, please don't hesitate to reach out."

Closing the Conversation
Nurse (You): "Remember, you're not alone. We're here to support you every step of the way. Take care, and we'll see you soon for your surgery."

KEY PHRASES TO USE

- "It's completely normal to feel scared before a surgery."
- "Many people feel the same way."
- "You're not alone, and we're here to support you."
- "Can you tell me more about what's making you feel anxious?"
- "Let me explain what will happen during the surgery."
- "The surgical team is very experienced and will take great care of you."
- "Most patients recover very well after this surgery."
- "Would you like to try a simple breathing exercise with me now?"
- "We'll arrange for a follow-up appointment after your surgery."
- "Remember, you're not alone. We're here to support you."

By using these strategies and phrases, you can effectively handle an anxious patient during an OET role play, demonstrating empathy, providing reassurance, and offering practical support.

Using empathetic sentences during the OET speaking session is crucial for demonstrating your ability to communicate compassionately and effectively with patients. Here are some empathetic sentences that can be used in various scenarios:

GENERAL EMPATHETIC SENTENCES

1. Acknowledging Feelings:
   - "I can see that you're feeling very upset right now."
   - "It sounds like you're really worried about this situation."
   - "I understand that this is a difficult time for you."
2. Showing Understanding:
   - "I can't imagine how hard this must be for you."
   - "It's completely normal to feel this way."
   - "I understand that you have concerns, and it's okay to feel that way."
3. Offering Reassurance:
   - "We're here to support you through this."
   - "You're not alone in this. We will get through it together."
   - "We'll do everything we can to help you manage this."

SPECIFIC SCENARIOS

Breaking Bad News

- Introducing the News:

"I'm afraid I have some difficult news to share with you."

- Delivering the News:

"I'm very sorry to tell you that your test results indicate [condition]."

- Responding to Emotions:
  - "I can see this news is very upsetting. It's okay to feel this way."
  - "This must be really hard for you to hear."

Handling Anxiety

- Acknowledge Anxiety:

"I understand that you're feeling very anxious about this procedure."

- Providing Comfort:

"Many patients feel the same way before a surgery. It's normal to be nervous."

- Offering Support:

"We'll take good care of you and make sure you're as comfortable as possible."

Handling Depression

- Recognizing Depression:

"I'm really sorry you're feeling this way. Depression can be very overwhelming."

- Encouraging Expression:

"Would you like to talk more about what's been making you feel this way?"

- Providing Hope:

"There are many resources and treatments available that can help you feel better."

Dealing with Sadness

- Acknowledging Sadness:

"I'm really sorry that you're feeling so sad."

- Validating Emotions:

"It's completely understandable to feel this way after what you've been through."

- Offering Support:

"We're here to help you and provide the support you need."

Handling Frustration

- Recognizing Frustration:

"I can see that you're feeling very frustrated."

- Validating Feelings:

"It's understandable to feel frustrated given the circumstances."

- Providing Solutions:

"Let's see what we can do to address your concerns."

EXAMPLE ROLE PLAY SCRIPT USING EMPATHETIC SENTENCES

Scenario:
You need to inform a patient about a serious diagnosis.

Nurse (You): "Hello [Patient's Name], my name is [Your Name], and I'm your nurse today. How are you feeling?"

Patient: "I'm feeling really anxious about my test results."

Nurse (You): "I understand that you're feeling very anxious, and it's completely normal to feel this way. I'm afraid I have some difficult news to share with you. Your test results have come back, and they indicate that you have [specific condition]. I'm very sorry to tell you this."

Patient: "This is so hard to hear. What does this mean for me?"

Nurse (You): "I can't imagine how difficult this must be for you. It's okay to feel shocked and upset right now. We are here to support you through this. There are many resources and treatments available that can help manage the condition and improve your quality of life. Would you like me to explain more about the condition and the treatment options available?"

Patient: "Yes, please. I need to know what happens next."

Nurse (You): "Of course. [Provide a brief explanation.] We'll also arrange for a follow-up appointment to discuss your treatment plan in detail and connect you with a specialist who can provide more information and support. Remember, you're not alone in this. We'll get through it together."

By incorporating these empathetic sentences, you can effectively communicate with patients in an OET speaking session, demonstrating your ability to provide compassionate and supportive care.

Using reassuring sentences during the OET speaking session helps to comfort and support patients, demonstrating your ability to communicate effectively and empathetically. Here are some reassuring sentences that can be used in various scenarios:

reassuring sentences used in oet speaking

GENERAL REASSURING SENTENCES

1. Providing General Reassurance:
   - "We're here to support you every step of the way."
   - "You're in good hands."
   - "We will do everything we can to help you feel better."
   - "You're not alone; we're here to help."
2. Offering Comfort:
   - "It's completely normal to feel this way."
   - "Many patients feel the same before [procedure/treatment]."
   - "We have a lot of experience with this, and you're going to be well taken care of."
3. Expressing Commitment:
   - "We're committed to making sure you get the best care possible."
   - "Your well-being is our top priority."
   - "We will monitor your progress closely and adjust as needed."

SPECIFIC SCENARIOS

Before a Procedure

- "It's normal to feel nervous before a procedure. We'll make sure you're comfortable throughout."
- "Our team is very experienced and will take great care of you."
- "We'll be with you every step of the way to ensure everything goes smoothly."

After Diagnosing a Condition

- "We have many effective treatments available, and we'll work together to manage this condition."
- "There are plenty of resources to help you through this."
- "We'll develop a treatment plan tailored to your needs."

During Treatment or Recovery

- "You're doing great. Keep following the treatment plan, and we'll see continued improvement."
- "Recovery takes time, but you're making good progress."
- "We're here to support you as you recover. If you have any questions or concerns, please let us know."

Dealing with Anxiety

- "I understand that you're feeling anxious, and that's completely normal. We're here to help you through it."
- "Let's take this one step at a time. We'll get through it together."

- "We have techniques that can help you manage your anxiety. Would you like to try some now?"

When the Patient is Sad or Depressed

- "It's okay to feel sad. We're here to support you."
- "We have resources and support systems to help you through this difficult time."
- "We'll work together to find the best ways to help you feel better."

EXAMPLE ROLE PLAY SCRIPT USING REASSURING SENTENCES

Scenario:
A patient is feeling anxious about an upcoming surgery.

Nurse (You): "Hello [Patient's Name], my name is [Your Name], and I'll be your nurse today. How are you feeling about your upcoming surgery?"

Patient: "I'm really nervous. I've never had surgery before."

Nurse (You): "It's completely normal to feel nervous before surgery, especially if it's your first time. We'll make sure you're comfortable throughout the procedure. Our team is very experienced and will take great care of you. You're in good hands."

Patient: "What if something goes wrong?"

Nurse (You): "I understand your concerns. We have a highly skilled team, and we take every precaution to ensure your safety. We'll be monitoring you closely during the surgery to make sure everything goes smoothly. You're not alone; we'll be with you every step of the way."

Patient: "That makes me feel a little better, but I'm still scared."

Nurse (You): "That's completely understandable. Let's take this one step at a time. If you'd like, we can practice some relaxation techniques now to help manage your anxiety. Remember, we're here to support you and ensure that you have the best possible care."

By incorporating these reassuring sentences, you can effectively communicate with patients in an OET speaking session, providing them with comfort and support while demonstrating your professional and empathetic communication skills.

Giving advice and recommendations is a crucial part of the OET speaking test, especially for nurses. Here are some example sentences you can use to effectively provide advice and recommendations in various scenarios:

GENERAL ADVICE AND RECOMMENDATIONS

1. Health and Lifestyle Advice:
    - "It's important to maintain a balanced diet. Eating a variety of fruits and vegetables can help improve your health."
    - "Regular exercise is beneficial. Aim for at least 30 minutes of moderate activity most days of the week."
    - "Make sure to stay hydrated by drinking plenty of water throughout the day."
2. Medication and Treatment:
    - "It's essential to take your medication as prescribed. If you have any questions about how to take it, please let me know."
    - "If you experience any side effects, contact your doctor immediately."
    - "Make sure to complete the full course of antibiotics even if you start feeling better."
3. Managing Symptoms:
    - "If you're experiencing pain, you can take over-the-counter pain relievers such as ibuprofen or acetaminophen."
    - "Applying a warm compress to the area can help reduce discomfort."
    - "Try to rest and avoid any strenuous activities while you're recovering."
4. Follow-Up Care:

- "It's important to attend all your follow-up appointments to monitor your progress."
- "If your symptoms persist or worsen, please contact the clinic immediately."
- "We recommend that you keep a diary of your symptoms to discuss at your next visit."

SPECIFIC SCENARIOS

Scenario: Patient with Hypertension

Nurse (You): "To help manage your blood pressure, it's important to reduce your salt intake. Try to avoid processed foods and add less salt when cooking. Also, regular physical activity, like brisk walking for 30 minutes a day, can significantly help in controlling your blood pressure."

Scenario: Patient Recovering from Surgery

Nurse (You): "After your surgery, it's crucial to get plenty of rest and avoid lifting heavy objects. Keep the surgical area clean and dry to prevent infection. If you notice any signs of infection, such as redness or swelling, please contact us immediately."

Scenario: Patient with Diabetes

Nurse (You): "Managing your blood sugar levels is essential. Make sure to check your blood sugar as directed and take your medication on time. A balanced diet with controlled carbohydrate intake and regular physical activity can help keep your blood sugar levels stable."

Scenario: Patient with Anxiety

Nurse (You): "Practicing relaxation techniques, such as deep breathing exercises or meditation, can help manage your anxiety. It's also helpful to establish a regular sleep routine and avoid caffeine, especially in the evening. If your anxiety persists, consider speaking to a counselor or therapist."

EXAMPLE ROLE PLAY SCRIPT USING ADVICE AND RECOMMENDATIONS

Scenario:

A patient with hypertension needs advice on lifestyle changes.

Nurse (You): "Hello [Patient's Name], my name is [Your Name], and I'm your nurse today. How are you feeling?"

Patient: "I'm feeling okay, but I'm worried about my high blood pressure."

Nurse (You): "It's good that you're thinking about managing your blood pressure. There are several lifestyle changes you can make to help control it. First, reducing your salt intake is very important. Try to avoid processed foods and don't add extra salt to your meals."

Patient: "Okay, I can do that. What else should I do?"

Nurse (You): "Regular physical activity is also very beneficial. Aim for at least 30 minutes of moderate exercise, like brisk walking, most days of the week. Additionally, maintaining a healthy weight, managing stress through relaxation techniques, and limiting alcohol intake can all help in managing your blood pressure."

Patient: "That sounds manageable. I'll start with these changes."

Nurse (You): "That's great to hear. It's also important to monitor your blood pressure regularly and keep track of your readings. If you notice any significant changes or have any concerns, please contact us. And don't forget to attend your follow-up appointments to keep an eye on your progress."

By using these example sentences and scenarios, you can effectively provide advice and recommendations to patients during an OET speaking session, demonstrating your ability to communicate clearly and supportively as a nurse.

Improving your English speaking skills, particularly for the OET (Occupational English Test), requires a combination of targeted practice, comprehensive resources, and effective strategies. Here are some resources and tips to help you improve:

COMMON WARM-UP QUESTIONS AND SUGGESTED ANSWERS

1. Tell me about your job.

Question: "Can you tell me about your job?" Answer: "Yes, of course. I am a registered nurse working in a community health clinic. My responsibilities include providing primary care to patients, administering medications, educating patients about their health conditions, and offering support for chronic disease management. I also work closely with doctors and other healthcare professionals to ensure comprehensive care for our patients."

2. Why did you choose to become a nurse/doctor?

Question: "Why did you choose to become a nurse?" Answer: "I chose to become a nurse because I have always been passionate about helping others. I find it rewarding to support patients through their health challenges and to make a positive impact on their lives. Additionally, I enjoy the variety and constant learning opportunities that the nursing profession offers."

3. What do you enjoy most about your job?

Question: "What do you enjoy most about your job?" Answer: "What I enjoy most about my job is the interaction with patients. Building relationships and seeing patients recover or manage their conditions successfully gives me a great sense of fulfillment. I also appreciate the collaborative environment and the chance to work with a dedicated team of healthcare professionals."

4. What are the common health issues you encounter in your job?

Question: "What are the common health issues you encounter in your job?"
Answer: "In my job, I frequently encounter health issues such as
hypertension, diabetes, respiratory infections, and chronic pain. We also see
a significant number of patients with mental health concerns, such as
anxiety and depression. Managing these conditions requires a holistic
approach and continuous patient education."

5. How do you handle stressful situations at work?

Question: "How do you handle stressful situations at work?" Answer:
"Handling stressful situations is part of the job, and I've developed several
strategies to manage stress effectively. I prioritize tasks to ensure that the
most critical needs are addressed first. I also practice deep breathing
exercises and take short breaks when possible to stay calm and focused.
Additionally, I rely on my colleagues for support and always try to maintain
a positive outlook."

6. What is the most challenging aspect of your job?

Question: "What is the most challenging aspect of your job?" Answer: "One
of the most challenging aspects of my job is dealing with emotional
situations, such as delivering bad news to patients or supporting families
during difficult times. It requires a great deal of empathy and emotional
resilience. However, I find that providing compassionate care and support
during these times is also one of the most important and rewarding parts of
my role."

TIPS FOR ANSWERING WARM-UP QUESTIONS

1. Be Clear and Concise: Provide clear and concise answers, avoiding overly long or complex responses.
2. Stay Relevant: Focus on aspects of your professional life that are relevant to the question and demonstrate your experience and skills.
3. Show Enthusiasm: Display a positive attitude and enthusiasm for your job. This helps to create a good impression.
4. Use Professional Language: Use appropriate professional language and terminology, but avoid jargon that might be confusing.
5. Be Honest: Be truthful in your responses, as authenticity helps to build rapport and trust with the interlocutor.
6. Practice: Practice common questions and answers to build confidence and fluency. Recording yourself and listening to your responses can help identify areas for improvement.

By preparing for these warm-up questions and practicing your responses, you can start your OET Speaking test with confidence and set a positive tone for the rest of the test.

ONLINE RESOURCES

1. Official OET Resources
   - OET Website: The official OET website provides sample test materials, practice tests, and preparation guides. Visit <u>OET Official Website</u>.
   - OET Preparation Course: Enroll in official OET preparation courses that offer structured lessons and practice.
2. OET-Specific Preparation Platforms
   - OET Online: Offers a range of preparation courses, practice tests, and study materials specifically designed for the OET.
   - E2Language: Provides comprehensive OET preparation courses, including live classes, practice tests, and feedback from expert tutors.
3. General English Improvement Platforms
   - BBC Learning English: Offers a variety of resources, including lessons on grammar, vocabulary, pronunciation, and real-life English usage.
   - Duolingo: A free language learning app that helps improve vocabulary and grammar through interactive exercises.
   - British Council Learn English: Provides resources for all aspects of English learning, including speaking practice, vocabulary building, and grammar exercises.
4. YouTube Channels
   - OET Preparation: Channels like E2 OET and Swoosh English offer video lessons and tips

specifically for OET candidates.
- English Learning Channels: Channels like BBC Learning English, Learn English with Emma, and English Addict provide practical lessons and tips for improving English speaking skills.

PRACTICE AND INTERACTION

1. Language Exchange Platforms
   - Tandem: Connects you with native English speakers for language exchange. You can practice speaking English with them while helping them with your native language.
   - HelloTalk: Another platform for language exchange, allowing you to practice speaking with native English speakers.
2. Online Tutoring
   - iTalki: Offers personalized English lessons with native speakers and experienced tutors. You can practice speaking and receive feedback on your performance.
   - Preply: Connects you with professional tutors who can help you prepare for the OET and improve your general English speaking skills.
3. Speaking Practice Groups
   - OET Forums and Study Groups: Join OET-specific forums and study groups on platforms like Facebook and Reddit to connect with other candidates and practice speaking.
   - Meetup: Look for English language conversation groups in your area or virtual meetups to practice speaking with others.

ADDITIONAL TIPS

1. Record Yourself: Practice speaking on different topics and record yourself. Listen to the recordings to identify areas for improvement.
2. Role Play: Engage in role-playing exercises, simulating various OET scenarios such as patient consultations and clinical communication.
3. Reading Aloud: Read medical articles, case studies, and dialogues aloud to improve your pronunciation, fluency, and medical vocabulary.
4. Flashcards: Use flashcards to build your medical vocabulary and practice using new terms in sentences.
5. Mock Tests: Regularly take mock OET speaking tests under timed conditions to build confidence and improve your performance.

By utilizing these resources and strategies, you can effectively improve your English speaking skills and prepare for the OET. Consistent practice and targeted preparation will help you achieve better results in your speaking test.

ABOUT THE AUTHOR

Jobin Thomas (Jobins Training)

Jobin Thomas is the managing director of Jobins Training, one of the leading OET/IELTS training providers in India and the UK. He holds a bachelor's and master's degree in English Language and Literature, as well as a nursing degree. An associate member of the Chartered Institute of Linguists (CIOL), his diverse academic background and professional experiences bring a unique perspective to his literary works.

www.ingramcontent.com/pod-product-compliance
Lightning Source LLC
Chambersburg PA
CBHW040907130726
48005CB00019BA/3010